We Are Beloved

"This little devotional was such a godsend. Sitting with the wisdom of the great Sr. Thea Bowman refreshed and renewed me each day because it was such a simple way to pray alongside a spiritual master and to take time to reconnect to God at each point throughout my day. I'm so grateful for the time I spent with this book!"

Shannon Wimp Schmidt

Cohost of *Plaid Skirts & Basic Black* podcast

"Sr. Thea was a bright light in this world and to the Church, and her words are a gift to use in prayer and a challenge to more fully practice the faith. This book is a must-read, must-use, must-pray-with, and I am glad it exists."

Katie Prejean McGrady

Host of the *Ave Explores* podcast and *The Katie McGrady Show* on SiriusXM

We Are Beloved

GREAT SPIRITUAL TEACHERS

30 DAYS WITH

Thea Bowman

Edited by Karianna Frey

AVE MARIA PRESS AVE Notre Dame, Indiana

Series editor: John Kirvan

Permissions information is listed on page 85.

Founded in 1865, Ave Maria Press is a ministry of the United States Province of Holy Cross.

www.avemariapress.com

Paperback: ISBN-13 978-1-64680-099-5

E-book: ISBN-13 978-1-64680-100-8

Cover image © 2021 Ann Burt, www.etsy.com/shop/AnnBurtDevotionalArt.

Cover and text design by Katherine Robinson.

Printed and bound in the United States of America.

Library of Congress Cataloging-in-Publication Data

Names: Bowman, Thea, author. | Frey, Karianna, editor.

Title: We are beloved : 30 days with Thea Bowman / edited by Karianna Frey.

Description: Notre Dame, Indiana : Ave Maria Press, [2021] | Series: Great spiritual teachers | Includes bibliographical references. | Summary: "This thirty-day devotional guide is based on the prophetic words of Servant of God Sr. Thea Bowman, a renowned Black Catholic evangelizer, teacher, writer, and singer. The text walks readers through reflections on the healing community of the church, the dignity of the human person, and our need for connection and reconciliation"-- Provided by publisher.

Identifiers: LCCN 2021032930 (print) | LCCN 2021032931 (ebook) | ISBN 9781646800995 (paperback) | ISBN 9781646801008 (ebook)

Subjects: LCSH: Meditations. | Catholic Church--Prayers and devotions. | BISAC: RELIGION / Spirituality | RELIGION / Meditations

Classification: LCC BX2182.3 .B69 2021 (print) | LCC BX2182.3 (ebook) | DDC 242--dc23

LC record available at https://lccn.loc.gov/2021032930

LC ebook record available at https://lccn.loc.gov/2021032931

Contents

Timeline

1958   US Bishops denounce racism in "Discrimination and the Christian Conscience"

1963   US Bishops issue "On Racial Harmony"

1963   Martin Luther King Jr. delivers his "I Have a Dream" speech on August 28 during the March on Washington

1964   Civil Rights Act outlaws racial discrimination in employment, schools, and public places

1965   Bishop Harold Robert Perry becomes the second Black Catholic bishop in the United States

1968   First Black Clergy Caucus meets in Detroit, Michigan

1972   Bowman completes her PhD at the Catholic University of America in Washington, DC

1979   US Bishops issue "Brothers and Sisters to Us"

1984   Black Bishops of the United States write a pastoral letter on evangelization, "What We Have Seen and Heard"

1985   National Black Catholic Congress is reestablished

1989   Bowman gives her iconic address to the US
        Conference of Catholic Bishops on June
        19

1990   Bowman dies on March 30

2018   The cause for Bowman's canonization is
        opened, and she is declared a Servant of
        God

2018   US Bishops issue pastoral letter against
        racism, "Open Wide Our Hearts"

WHO IS

Thea Bowman?

Thea Bowman was born in 1937 and given the name Bertha Elizabeth Bowman. Raised in a Protestant family in Canton, Mississippi, Bowman was steeped in the richness of her Black culture and spirituality. Bowman attended Holy Child Jesus Church and School in Canton, and inspired by the examples of the Franciscan Sisters of Perpetual Adoration and the Missionary Servants of the Most Holy Trinity, she converted to Catholicism as a child.

Bowman was only fifteen when she decided to join the Franciscan Sisters of Perpetual Adoration, where she would be the only Black member of her religious community in Wisconsin. At her religious profession, she took the name, "Sister Mary Thea" in honor of the Blessed Mother and her father, Theon; she became known to many as simply "Sister Thea." She attended college at Viterbo University in Wisconsin, then went on to earn her master's degree and doctorate at the Catholic University of America in Washington, DC. Bowman finished her PhD in 1972 and began teaching at CUA, then returned to teach at Viterbo. She also taught at Xavier University of Louisiana in New Orleans and helped found its Institute for Black Catholics Studies.

Bowman became a popular and in-demand preacher, with more than one hundred engagements a year in the United States and abroad. Her dynamic appearances included spontaneous song and highlighted the joy of diversity and the demands of unity in Christ. She contributed to the landmark hymnal *Lead Me, Guide Me* which was the first collection that highlighted Black spirituality and culture.

Even after a diagnosis of breast cancer, Bowman continued to speak widely and joyfully. In 1989, she became the first Black woman to address the US Conference of Catholic Bishops, and she took the opportunity to share what it meant to be fully Black, and fully Catholic.

Reflecting on the richness of Black history and spirituality, Bowman stated:

> I bring myself; my black self, all that I am, all that I have, all that I hope to become. I bring my whole history, my traditions, my experience, my culture, my African-American song and dance and gesture and movement and teaching and preaching and healing and responsibility— as gifts to the Church. I bring a spirituality that our Black-American bishops told us (they just told us what everybody who knew, knew), that spirituality is contemplative and biblical and holistic, bringing to religion a totality of mind and imagination, of memory, of feeling and passion, and emotion and intensity. A faith that is embodied incarnate praise—a spirituality that knows how to find joy even in the time of sorrow—that steps out on faith that leans on the Lord.[1]

Bowman urged the bishops to respect the diversity of Black worship traditions and to work for greater inclusivity of Black lay and religious within the Church. She concluded her address by inviting the bishops to join her in singing "We Shall Overcome," an anthem of the civil rights movement. They did so, and then offered a thunderous applause.

Bowman died less than a year later, on March 30, 1990. She was posthumously awarded the University of Notre Dame's Laetare Medal, the oldest and most prestigious award for American Catholics. Bowman's legacy is upheld by the Sister Thea Bowman Black Catholic Educational Foundation, as well as through initiatives named in her honor across the United States. Her cause for canonization was opened in 2018, and she was declared Servant of God.

HOW TO

Use This Book

The books in the Great Spiritual Teacher series provide an introduction to the spiritual insights and wisdom of some of history's most extraordinary saints. Through these pages, you're invited to a place beyond mere reading, into an experience of daily prayer and meditation. You'll be accompanied by a spiritual teacher whose wisdom will awaken, enrich, and empower your walk with the Lord.

In other words, these books take you on a spiritual journey.

We have some suggestions for how you can make the most of this journey. But keep in mind that these books are meant to help you experience the freedom and joy of communing with God in prayer. The daily format is there to help—but don't hesitate to go at your own pace or take your own route! Repeat a day as often as you like, or skip a day if the reading isn't resonating with where you are in your journey. The goal is to hear the voice of God through the words of the saints.

However you choose to use this book, it's helpful to understand the thinking behind the format used for each day. We've chosen to follow the suggestion of the classic book on spirituality *The Cloud of Unknowing,* which describes a three-part movement of *reading, reflecting,* and *praying:* "These three are so linked together that there can be no profitable reflection without first reading or hearing. Nor will beginners or even the spiritually adept come to true prayer without first taking time to reflect on what they have heard or read."

Throughout these thirty days you'll follow in the footsteps of this longstanding tradition. Each day starts with a section called "My Day Begins," in which you'll find a passage quoted or adapted from a great spiritual teacher. This is followed by "All Through the Day," which provides a short, memorable phrase (drawn from or based on the reading) that you can carry with you throughout the day, enabling you to reflect and meditate on a key truth, question, or insight. In the final section, "My Day Is Ending," you're encouraged to find a quiet place to go to the Lord in prayer, drawing on that day's reading as you lift up your petitions and praises to him.

My Day Begins

One of the best ways you can begin your day is to put yourself in the company of a great spiritual teacher.

The selected passages are short—just a few hundred words. But they are powerful! They've been chosen specifically for their ability to provide spiritual focus for your day and to remind you that you are a spiritual being, intended for relationship and intimacy with God.

These morning readings don't just put you in the presence of a spiritual teacher who can accompany you on your journey—they are also designed to invite you into God's presence so you can start your day in conversation with him.

If you find that you don't fully understand the reading, don't be discouraged! Understanding may come with time, meditation, and further prayer. For now, focus on your heart's response. Tell the Lord about the questions you have, and ask him for wisdom and insight.

It's also helpful to read *slowly*. We've divided the passages into sense lines to help you do just that. Instead of rushing through the reading, savor each word. Pay attention to which phrases or images resonate in your heart. Make room for God to speak. In short, read prayerfully. Each day's opening reading is meant to foster attentiveness to God and an attitude of readiness to hear what he wants to say to you.

All Through the Day

After the day's reading you'll find a single sentence, a meditation that you can reflect on throughout your day. As you move forward with the busyness of everyday life, return to this reflection as often as you can. Try writing it down on a card and placing it somewhere you'll see it frequently. Or copy it down in a journal or planner. Recite it in the little free moments between tasks and conversations.

This reflection shouldn't take you out of the day's responsibilities. Rather, it should serve as a gentle reminder of God's presence within the many activities and tasks that make up your day—and an expression of your desire to live in connection with him.

My Day Is Ending

No matter what your day has brought to you, there's great wisdom in reaching the end of it and turning everything over to God in prayer, intentionally setting your mind and heart on him, and listening for his voice.

If you find that it's not easy to let go of the events of the day, to find peace and closure and solace in God's presence, here are some suggestions to help you:

1. Find a quiet, distraction-free place that you can return to each evening.

2. Quiet your spirit. Sometimes this involves relaxing your body and letting go of physical tension. Try adopting a posture that reminds you that you are in God's presence: sit or kneel; fold your hands or lift them up—whatever works for you. Focus on breathing deeply and deliberately.

3. When you feel calm and at peace, focus on the evening prayer phrase by phrase. If you find yourself getting caught up in analyzing the words of the prayer, wrestling with the meaning of a phrase, or becoming distracted, don't worry! Just pause, breathe, and begin again. Set aside all the distractions and worries that stand between you and God.

The time spent with the evening prayer doesn't need to be very long—just remember that it is a time of expressing complete trust and confidence in God, preparing yourself for a night of peaceful sleep. End the day as you began it, resting in his presence.

Some Other Ways to Use This Book

1. *Create your own reflections.* If the provided "All Through the Day" reflection doesn't resonate with you, or if you'd like to add to it, feel free to choose another phrase or image from the morning reading that caught your attention.

2. *Incorporate journaling into your spiritual journey.* Many find that journaling—either through copying out the provided reflections and prayers or writing your own—is an excellent way to slow down and focus, ensuring that your mind doesn't skip over important insights. Or you could use a journal to keep a record of your experiences on this thirty-day journey, such as the insights that had the biggest impact on your thinking, or any daily changes you noticed in your heart or behavior.

3. *Look for contrasts.* Sometimes two readings or reflections might seem to stand in tension with each other. Often, such tensions highlight areas for fruitful reflection. Write down the contrasting passages and any

THIRTY DAYS WITH

Thea Bowman

DAY 1

....

My Day Begins

"I'm an old folks child, and I never realized until I was grown up how well they taught me values, how well they taught me survival skills: how to face life, how to face pain, how to face death, how not to be scared, and if you're scared that don't make no difference, just as long as you keep on steppin'."[2]

Old folks used to say,
"God is bread when you're hungry.
God is water when you're thirsty.
God is shelter from the storm.
God is rest when you're weary.
God's my doctor.
God's my lawyer.
God's my captain who never lost a battle.
God is my lily of the valley."[3]

Old people in the black community taught us that we should serve the Lord until we die. We can even serve the Lord on our deathbed or in any circumstances in life. If we have faith, hope, and love we can pass it on. If we

work together, pray and stand together, we can create a
new heaven and ease life for each other.[4]

All Through the Day

Lord, show yourself to me in the people I meet today.

My Day Is Ending

Father, your sacred scripture promises that if I first
seek your kingdom and your righteousness, you will
provide all that I need.
I know that your Word is true and that you always keep
your promises, rendering powerless the lies the evil
one whispers into my ear in an effort to lead me into
doubt and despair.
I know that you will never let me fall, no matter how
strong the winds of disappointment, self-defeat,
jealousy, and pride rage around me.
Just as the winds on the Sea of Galilee stopped at your
command, your Word will still the winds that whirl
around me.
You call me into communion with you through your
sacred Word, when you proclaimed "I will not now call

you servants: for the servant knoweth not what his lord doth. But I have called you friends: because all things whatsoever I have heard of my Father, I have made known to you" (Jn 15:151).

You call me into communion with you through worship, when you sacrificed your life for mine for the redemption of my sins.

You call me into communion with you through community when I meet you in my friends, my enemies, my neighbor, and love them as I love myself.

Through your Word, worship, and community, I meet you every day of my life.

As long as I keep my eyes fixed on you, I will be alright. Amen.

My Day Begins

My people sang the songs of faith.
Songs of Adam and Eve,
Cain and Abel,
Noah, Moses, David,
And Jesus.
The songs of faith were passed on,
Taught, learned, and prayed
In an environment of love and celebration.

I did not realize I was receiving a religious education—that I was being taught prayer, salvation history, morals and values, faith, hope, love, and joy. I did not realize that the songs would form the basis of my lifelong religious education.

I did not realize that the songs would bring to me and to those I love comfort in sorrow, solace in grief, refuge in time of trouble, relief even from physical pain—always strength and hope, peace and joy.

Each spiritual is in its own way a prayer—of yearning or celebration, of praise, petition, or contemplation, a simple lifting of heart, mind, voice, and life to God.[5]

All Through the Day

I sing because I'm happy, I sing because I'm free.[6]

My Day Is Ending

Father, you have given us the gift of song to delight,
to learn, to share, and to love.
While I may not be able to have your Word in my
hands at all times,
I can hold your Word in my heart through song,
I can sing when I am happy.
I can sing when I am sad.
I can sing when I need to feel close to you.
Lord God, may I never fear to sing your praises.
Blessed be God who created and longed for commu-
nion with Adam and Eve.
Blessed be God who sought after Abel and rightly
judged Cain for his sin.
Blessed be God who spared Noah and his family and
renewed the face of the Earth.
Blessed be God who raised up Moses to walk His peo-
ple out from bondage.

Blessed be God who anointed David to be a shepherd
of men.
Blessed be God who became Jesus Christ, true God,
and true man, to become sin for us, who knew no sin,
so that we may live eternally in communion with him.
Amen.

DAY 3

....

My Day Begins

Proud, strong men and women, artists, teachers, healers, warriors and dream makers, inventors, and builders, administrators . . . politicians, priests: They came to these shores in the slave trade. Those who survived the indignity of the middle passage came to the American continents bringing treasures of African heritage: African spiritual and cultural gifts, wisdom, faith, and faithfulness, art and drama.[7]

When I was growing up, many of the old women who had undergone the ignominy of slavery were around, and they told us about slavery because they said we had to know about freedom.[8]

All Through the Day

Christ has made me free.

My Day Is Ending

Dearest Jesus, because of what you sacrificed for me, I am no longer a slave.

I am no longer a slave to opinion as my identity lies in my relationship with you.

I am no longer a slave to others as earthly whims and fancies hold no power or dominion over me.

I am no longer a slave to the world as you are the only king I choose to serve.

I am a child of the Most High.

I share in the inheritance promised to Abraham.

Through Abraham's faith, he knew that your promises are always kept and that his descendants would indeed number the stars.

Thank you, my Lord, for freeing me from bondage.

Thank you, my Lord for the freedom to share the Good News of your life, death, and resurrection with all those I meet.

Thank you, my Lord, for freeing me from the burdens that I place upon my shoulders, by taking them and carrying them for me.

Thank you, my Lord, for sending Your Spirit to console me when I feel I cannot take another step forward.

Thank you, my Lord, for giving me the words of life to
speak into another.
Thank you, my Lord, for loving me just as I am.
Amen.

My Day Begins

If we are to serve, if we are to care,
if we are to minister,
we have to get right inside.
And so, let us pray: Spirit, touch me.
Touch me with your grace,
Touch me with your wisdom.
Touch me with your love so that I can help somebody,
so that I can serve somebody,
so that I can bless somebody.
Be the bridge over troubled waters, so that I can be the
balm in Gilead,
be the hands of Jesus stretched out to heal.[9]

If I can help somebody as I pass along, then my living will not be in vain. Let us meditate on those words and carry them in our hearts and carry them into our homes, into our neighborhoods, and teach them to our children.[10]

Let us be practical, reaching out across the boundaries of race and class and status to help somebody, to encourage and affirm somebody, offering to the young an incentive to learn and grow, offering to the downtrodden resources to help themselves. May our fasting be the kind that saves and shares with the poor, that actually contacts the needy, that gives heart to heart, that touches and nourishes and heals.[11]

All Through the Day

Spirit, help me see through the eyes of Jesus.

My Day Is Ending

Loving Father, too often I hold myself apart from others, not because I do not care, but because I do not want to get hurt.
I do not want to face rejection.
I do not want to see the humanity in another because they might see the humanity in me. I do not want to get in so deep that I might not make it out.
I do not want to feel the emotional pain of another when I can barely deal with my own emotional pain.
While I know that I was never guaranteed comfort when I picked up my cross to follow you, I also do not go seeking discomfort willingly.
Help me to move outside of myself,
to love more like you loved,
to serve more like you served,

and to be willing to lay my life down for another
as you laid down your life for me.
Give me courage to not only look the homeless in the
eye, but to also ask them how they are doing or if they
have had a hot meal that day.
Give me the strength to speak boldly about you and
your love for me. Let me share how choosing to follow
you has changed my life.
Be with me as I reach out to someone who is suffering
and take some of their suffering onto my shoulders.
Lord, you call us to be your hands and your feet.
Grant me the grace to actually do so.
Amen.

DAY 5

....

My Day Begins

Some of us are poor. Some of us have not had the advantages of education. But how can people still have a voice and a role in the work of the church? Isn't that what the church is calling us all to?[12]

We're called to walk together in a new way toward that land of promise and to celebrate who we are and whose we are. If we as church walk together, don't let nobody separate you. . . . The church teaches us that the church is a family. It is a family of families and the family got to stay together. We know that if we do stay together, if we walk and talk and work and play and stand together in Jesus' name, we'll be who we say we are, truly Catholic; and we shall overcome.[13]

Look inside yourself; look into your heart; look into your life, remember the people who brought you in faith and taught you in faith, who led and fed you in faith . . . the ones who led you in the storm, who set a welcoming table for you, who taught you to say "precious Lord take my hand," who convinced you that you were God's child when the whole world told you you were nobody and would amount to nothing.[14]

All Through the Day

I am a beloved child of God.

My Day Is Ending

Abba, Father:
Thank you for the gift of faith of those around me.
You have placed witnesses in my life: parents who
have guided my steps, teachers who have encouraged
and inspired me, and friends who have challenged me.
These people remind me that not only am I a
child of God,
but that I am so beloved in the eyes of the Father.
But, Father, humans are not perfect and do not always
live up to our expectations.
And in the absence of those to inspire us here on Earth,
you have given us a cloud of witnesses in the communion of saints to always walk alongside of us. Your
Blessed Mother is my mother. Heavenly Father, you
are my Father. Your earthly father is an example of
unconditional love, and all of the saints are
my teachers and friends.
Make me more aware of when you are calling me

to lead others in the storm,
to be a place of welcome and refuge,
and to show another that they too are a beloved child
of God. Send your Spirit down upon me to give me the
words that you speak into the heart of one who is seeking, lost, or suffering.

Amen.

DAY 6

∙∙

My Day Begins

Look at the word *family*. See how the life of community and Church radiate from family. If we nurture faith, values, and love in the family, then we can nurture faith, values, and love in the community and the Church.

Family is the basic raw material from which community and Church can be formed. Family is the model of Church.

Traditions and rituals of family, community, and Church embody faith, values, and love and provide life-giving connection with our past, vitality and comfort to our present, and hope and courage for our future.

Families giving life, nurturing, nourishing, supporting, sustaining, encoding values, breaking bread, giving, forgiving . . . worshipping the Lord with heart and soul, sharing bread and Eucharist, strengthening family unity through Faith and Sacrament, witnessing the Good News of Christ the Liberator, working to bring about the coming of the Kingdom, feeding the hungry, sheltering the homeless, walking in solidarity with the oppressed and poor, signaling the eschatological reality of God's love, challenging one another and challenging the Church to be truly Christian, truly Catholic.[15]

All Through the Day

Love starts with family.

My Day Is Ending

Father, you brought love into the world
through a family.
Family is more than mother, father, brother, and sister.
Family is chosen and given, and it is through our families that we learn how to love as you call us to love.
You loved us so much that you became God incarnate
to be as one with us.
You were born into a family and played with cousins
and friends as you grew up.
You are the King of the Universe, and yet, you chose to
spend time with fishermen, tax collectors, lepers,
and women.
You communed with the voiceless, the powerless,
those on the margins of society, because only they
would have the humility to not only listen but to hear
and share your message of unconditional love.

You taught that love of God is radical, complete, and
never-ending and that true love can only come from
the inside.
You taught that love of neighbor first has to start with
love of self because we are called to love our neighbors
as ourselves.
Help me to be family to those around me, help me to
love everyone I meet as part of your family. Amen.

DAY 7

My Day Begins

How can we love and embrace the lonely, the fearful, the homeless, the outcast, the rejected, the unwanted the unrecognized, the poor? How can we witness to the Good News that we are walking together toward Canaan in love?[16]

You have a gift. You have a talent. Find your gift, find your talent and use it. You can make this world better just by letting your light shine and doing your part. You can help somebody just by caring about somebody, just by loving somebody. And then when you get through show them how much you love them, sometimes folks need to hear it, so make sure you tell them, I love you, I love you, I love you. I really, really, really, really love you!

That's all we've got to do: love the Lord, to love our neighbor. Amen. Amen. Amen. Amen.[17]

All Through the Day

This little light of mine, I'm gonna let it shine![18]

My Day Is Ending

Dearest Lord, the evil one likes to tell me that I'm not
good enough.
I see the message in social media postings, in adver-
tisements, in denied promotions, failed ventures, and
broken relationships.
I hear it in the mocking laughter of those who have no
faith, in the words of derision that cut like a knife into
my heart.
The moment that I begin to compare myself to another
is when I place a barrier between me and my friend
and I begin to believe the lies.
The lies that say that my gifts are worthless, that my
gifts are meaningless, or worse, that I have no gifts.
The lies that say that I am not trying hard enough, that
if I was perfect then everything would be right in my
world. That, in the opinion of the world,
I am not worthy.
The evil one is the master manipulator who weaves in
small truths into his insidious lies and those lies pre-
vent me from doing your will.
Help me to always remember that I have gifts to share
because I am your creation, created me out of love to
share love, and my gifts come directly from God.

I reject the lies of the evil one and I will shine your light in me for all to see. Amen.

• •

My Day Begins

It was the witness of Catholic Christians who were really making a difference in people's loves that made me interested in the Catholic Church.

I have to assume the responsibility of reaching out to my sisters and my brothers, and as I reach out, I take my friends with me. I introduce my friends to my friends. We begin to work together being Church. We are the Church!

When we come together in Jesus' name to do the work of the Church, when we come together as Church to worship and praise, to preach and teach, to feed the hungry, to clothe the naked, to teach the children . . . when we reach out to the lonely and the alienated and the afflicted . . . we don't realize that we are the Church and we are doing the work of the Church. . . .

The Church is more than a body of believers in the Lord—it is an extended family. The Faith is lived by the people, enlivened by spirituality, and responsive to their needs.[19]

All Through the Day

Father, I am your hands and feet. I am your Church.

My Day Is Ending

Father, there are days when the work seems just
impossible, the mission field too broad.
There is so much suffering: communities without clean
water, families without access to health care, people
struggling with mental illness, both diagnosed
and undiagnosed.
There is so much poverty: people living in food des-
erts, living without running water, living one missed
paycheck away from homelessness.
There is so much despair: people feeling unwanted,
unseen, unloved because of the color of their skin,
their history, their personal demons.
We see neighbor against neighbor, friend against
friend, families torn apart.
When we look out and see what needs to be done, our
spirits fall because there is no way that we can possibly
help everyone.
We are called to be your hands and your feet and we do
not work alone.

When I chose to walk with you, sweet Jesus, I became
part of a larger community, a larger family; I became
part of your Church.
Your Church does not and should not work in isolation.
When we all come together to do our little part, the
impossible becomes possible because "with God all
things are possible" (Mt 19:26). Amen.

DAY 9

....

My Day Begins

The well was deep, and he had no bucket. Jews did not ordinarily talk with Samaritans. Rabbis did not ordinarily speak with women in public. Holy people did not ordinarily consort with public sinners. But Jesus said to her, "Give me to drink." He asked her for a favor. He engaged her in conversation. He helped her to identify her own weaknesses and her strength. She gave him water from the well that was her Samaria. He, in return, gave her water that became in her a spring of living water giving eternal life. She gave him herself as she was, without subterfuge or guile. He healed her guilt and restored her vitality. He transformed her and used her to bring not being all of Samaria to his feet.

When I acknowledge myself—my true self—weak, failing, incomplete, inconsequential, yet gifted and capable of transcendence; when I accept my neediness and come just as I am, I too can recognize the Messiah, and with joy I shall go running to my city crying, "Come! Come! Come, see a Man told me everything I have done!"[20]

All Through the Day

Lord, show me my true self.

My Day Is Ending

Lord, you know the truth of self that I would prefer no
one else know or see.
You know how I hide my sinfulness and the messy
parts to fit in with the ideal image that I have created
in my head.
You know when I play the part of having everything
together, at least for a little while, to show others that
the Christian life is not hard to live.
You know the way that I fool others as much as
I fool myself.
You know when I am seeking the acceptance of the
world rather than reveling in the unconditional love
of you.
You see when I am fixated on following the law rather
than picking up my cross and following you.
I pray for the courage to celebrate the glory of your creation in me to the world around—my true self in all of
its messiness and imperfections.

When you told the woman at the well all that she had
done, she did not react with shame or despair, but with
joy at seeing and meeting you.

You saw her true self and with that relationship, gave
her permission to let others see her true self, to come
into intimacy with others. With your words in her
heart, she allowed her walls to come down
and to be vulnerable.

I want the same joy that the woman at the well shared,
the joy that comes from letting my walls down, expos-
ing my true self, becoming more vulnerable, and allowing you to fully come to dwell within me. Amen.

DAY 10

···

My Day Begins

If we are to serve, if we are to care, if we are to minister, we have to get right inside. And so let us pray: Spirit, touch me. Touch me with your grace. Touch me with your wisdom. Touch me with your love so that I can help somebody, so that I can serve somebody. Be the bridge over troubled waters so that I can be the balm in Gilead, be the hands of Jesus stretched out to heal.

Children, Mothers, Fathers, Sisters, Brothers, go! There is a song that will never be sung unless you sing it. There is a story that will never be told unless you tell it. There is a joy that will never be shared unless you bear it.

Go tell the world. Go preach the Gospel. Go teach the Good News.

God is. God is love. God is with us. God is in our lives.[21]

All Through the Day

I am a witness to the Good News.

My Day Is Ending

My God, yours is a story of love; a love so deep that
you consented to be born of a woman, our Emmanuel,
God with us.

You grew, you called, you taught, you led, and you
were willing to sacrifice your human body for the
redemption of my eternal soul. Our Jesus, God saves.
Like your beloved disciples who could not stay awake
while you agonized in the garden, I would rather
choose to seek comfort than to do the hard work in
service to you. Grant me the grace to be willing to sacrifice my comfort to help those around me to be a little
more comfortable on this journey home to You
in heaven.

The Roman scourges tore away your flesh, bit by bit,
dropping your holy blood to the ground, just like when
words intended to inflict pain on another, pass over my
lips. Help me to speak the words of life into another,
and reject hateful and harmful words.

When you fed the multitudes at the Sea of Galilee,
the adoring crowds wanted to make you a king, but
the only crown that you would accept was a crown
of thorns as the soldiers mocked you. Give me your

strength to share your love with others, and help me
to overcome my fear of being mocked and ridiculed by
those around me.

Our Blessed Mother watched as you carried the Cross
for me and my sins. You were innocent and you carried your Cross for the guilty. You carried your Cross
for me. Through the actions of saints Simon and Veron-
ica, I can see how I too have a part to play in your
gift of salvation by being a witness to the Good News.

Amen.

DAY 11

....

My Day Begins

Cast out of paradise, exiled and troubled, humanity
longed for *home.*
Brought out of Egypt, wandering through the desert
and wilderness, God's people longed for *home*, the
Promised Land across Jordan that would flow with
milk and honey.
In the days of slavery, separated from kin and country,
my ancestors longed for *home.*
I grew up in that kind of world in which life and death
was part of the cycle of reality, that was a part of God's
plan that was good. . . . Time doesn't really matter.
When it is over, it will be all over. I want people who
love me to know that I tried to choose life, and I did it
for myself, but I also did it for them.
With the little time you have, you have to live it well;
you have to live the best you can.[22]

All Through the Day

Take my hand, precious Lord, lead me home.[23]

My Day Is Ending

Precious Lord, I know that my time here on Earth is
finite and that I was not created to be of this world.
Give me the strength to keep my eyes fixed on you,
especially when things get hard. It is hard to admit that
I am not perfect. It is hard to acknowledge that I can
and have hurt others.

It's hard to see things through the eyes of another. It
is hard to see injustice taking place in your name. It is
hard to see Christianity turned into something
that it is not.

Taking up my cross and following you demands change
in me.

Every day when I wake up, I make the decision to turn
away from what is easy or convenient or comfortable.
In giving us the gift of free will, you have given us the
gift of saying no . . . we have the gift of humanity. By
learning how to say no and how to say yes at the right
times, I can better serve others through serving you.

Help me to remember that my final home is with you, your sweet Mother, all of the angels and saints and when my work here is done I will hear those words of love, "Well done, good and faithful servant" (Mt 25:23).

Amen.

DAY 12

My Day Begins

I walk in a number of different communities, just like my Native American brothers and sisters and my Hispanic brothers and sisters, my Asian brothers and sisters; we have to walk in more than one world. . . . I have to be bilingual, bicultural. I have to be able to talk your talk and talk it better than you can if I am going to be accepted and respected by many people in your society.

When we come together from our various spiritual perspectives, we learn from one another. From my Native sisters I learn a spirituality that lives in harmony with nature and with nature's God. I learn African ways of expressing feelings and passions and emotions and frustrations and yearnings influenced by the ignominy of the passage and our experience of slavery in the Americas.[24]

All Through the Day

Open my eyes to the experiences of others to help me see your truth.

My Day Is Ending

Father in heaven, I can know nothing on my own and I thank you for the wondrous gift of diversity in your creation. While we all look, sound, and worship differently, your love for humanity is a story that extends beyond human limitations and understanding.

The diversity of each of our stories and lives is strengthened by the love evident in your gospel. The diversity of your creation is all around us as we are all created in your image.

Each of us has dignity and worth because you created us with dignity and worth. No human is worth more than another, no human is superior to another because we are all your image-bearers.

Diversity in the Church reflects the diversity described in scripture from Genesis to Revelation, a story through which we see God becoming a man to redeem the sins of all of us.

It is a story of God creating a people for himself from all of the peoples in every nation. It is through the inclusion of others that we begin to see each other, learn from each other, fully love each other.

Diversity reminds us that we are made for communion and that communion is intentional because it requires action on my part to seek diversity. Because you dwell in each and every one of us, you are each and every one of us. Grant us the grace to lay our pride on the altar for your glory and honor. Amen.

DAY 13

....

My Day Begins

Our history includes the services of a Simon of Cyrene, the search of that Ethiopian eunuch; the contributions of Black Egypt in art, mathematics, monasticism, and politics; the art and architecture of Zimbabwe; the scholarship of Timbuktu; the dignity and serenity of textile, gold work, and religion in Ghana; the pervasive spirituality and vitality of Nigeria; the political and social systems of Zaire. Our history includes enslavements, oppression, and exploitation.

Our history is power. We can learn from it. We don't need to make all the mistakes ourselves. If we remember the misery of slavery, the struggles for freedom and Civil Rights, the joys of the past, if we remember how far we have come, our memory is power.

When we know ourselves, we bring the gift of our history and our culture to one another, to the Church, and to the world.[25]

All Through the Day

Father, may I never forget our history.

My Day Is Ending

Dearest Jesus, we live in a time when we would rather forget the pains of the past, or pretend that the events of the past never happened.

It is uncomfortable to remember when Black Americans were enslaved for the benefit and comfort of their white landowners.

We refuse to see the human trafficking happening before our eyes, fueled by our desire for sinful acts.

It is shameful to remember how immigrants were forced to, and currently, live in squalor and work for low wages and no job security.

Just as it is painful to acknowledge the holocaust of Jewish families by Nazi Germany, it is also difficult to acknowledge the actions of Catholics during the Spanish Inquisition.

It makes us uneasy to think about the negative effects that the Spanish mission system and native land loss had on Indigenous Americans,

all in the name of sharing the Gospel.

May I always remember the past, not to be caught up in it, but to learn from it.

Grant me the grace to see the memories of the past not as something to be covered up, ashamed of, or canceled, but as memories of the power that comes from you, allowing me to overcome the challenges that loom before me now. Amen.

DAY 14

My Day Begins

Children close to the heart of a Family, Community, Church respond and remain constant to the values of Family, Community, Church.[26]

Just because you are ten years old, don't think I'm not talking to you, and you are never too old to love.

To affirm the child because of his own worth; to look at the child and love the child and tell the child, "If anybody asks you who you are, just tell them you're a child of God. I may be poor but I am somebody. . . . You might think I'm slow, but I am somebody. I'm God's child."[27]

All Through the Day

I am somebody. I am God's child.

My Day Is Ending

Lord Jesus, you could have come into the world as the king you are, full of power and majesty.

Instead you came into the world as a poor, defenseless child and you reminded your apostles that our faith needs to be like that of a child; that to experience the kingdom of heaven,
we need to have the humility of a child.
We must ask questions to help us better understand your Church, and to refrain from being ignorant of the truth. We must want to seek knowledge of you through your holy scriptures and Church tradition. We must maintain the childlike qualities that the world seeks to beat out of us; the qualities of joy, wonder, awe, imagination, openness with our feelings, hope, trust, energy, forgiveness, and most of all, love.
Unlike others around you, you not only valued children, but you elevated the child when you told us "whoever takes the lowly position of this child is the greatest in the kingdom of heaven" (Mt 18:4, NIV). You lived in awe of life, in awe of God the Father, and in awe of humanity. To everyone else, I may be nobody, but to you I am somebody because I am, and always will be, your child. Amen.

....

My Day Begins

Everybody needs family. We start with a basic human need for family and for one another. We realize that one father, one mother are not enough: that families need the support of other families, and so we seek ways of bonding, nourishing, and healing.

We become community when families share values and needs. This bonding strengthens and nourishes us. That love that makes us community also makes us truly Church.

Family feeds the Church and Church necessarily feeds family. If we're not Church at home, we can't be Church when we go to church. If we are not family, we can't become Church.[28]

All Through the Day

Lord, may I treat my family the same way I treat those at Church.

My Day Is Ending

Lord Jesus, it is hard to love the people around
me sometimes.

It's so much easier to be nice to people when I only
have to see them once a week. Your Word reminds me
that it is in loving our brothers and sisters that we fully
love you.

Help me to remember that I am Christian not just
on Sundays, but every day of the week and that the
Church is more than the building where I pray.

Help me to remember that my home is also a sanctu-
ary, a sacred space for you. Grant me the grace to be an
effective gatekeeper to my home, help me to cover my
home in prayer.

As I walk through the rooms of my home, may I always
remember your presence with me and my family.

Fill the hearts of my family with peace and love,
crowding out annoyance and anger, and that the peace
and love that we experience at home spills out to our
workplaces, schools, neighborhoods, and surrounding
communities. Help me to find joy in the mundane;
may my daily tasks become symphonies of praise.

Thank you, Lord, for the provision of a home. My
home may not be the biggest or the fanciest or the
best decorated, but it provides shelter and protection

to my family, and I consecrate it to you for your glory.
Protect my home from evil influence, against fear,
pornography, deception, lies, and angry words. Thank
you, Lord, for my daily bread, both in the food that
nourishes me physically and the gift of the Eucharist to
nourish me spiritually.

Help us to become humble and gentle, patient with
one another in love, and united with the Spirit through
the bond of peace. May my home be a place of peace,
love, and worship of you all the days of my life. Amen.

DAY 16

. . . .

My Day Begins

The old ladies say that if you love the Lord you God with your whole heart, [with] your whole soul and your whole mind and all your strength, then you praise the Lord with your whole heart and soul and mind and strength and you don't bring Him any feeble service.[29]

The Word of God became Incarnate. We are called to preach that word day by day by day—in our homes, in our families, in our neighborhoods—to bear witness, to testify, to shout it from the rooftops with our lives. God has called us to speak the word that is Christ, that is truth, that is salvation. And if we speak that word in love and faith, with patience and prayer and perseverance, it will take root.[30]

All Through the Day

Ev'ry time I feel the Spirit movin', I pray![31]

My Day Is Ending

Father, please give me the strength to never be embar-
rassed to let others know that I belong to you.
Send your Spirit upon me so that I can shine your light
to illuminate the darkness around me. Do not let me
hide your light in fear of giving offense or making others uncomfortable by my actions. Help me to see the
Beatitudes as more than just instructions to live life,
but as a call to action.
I am poor in Spirit when I offer time to you in daily
prayer and in service to others. To those who mourn,
may I reach out with words of comfort and with offers
to ease their burdens and may I accept offers of help
when I am in need.
I acknowledge my humility and meekness when I not
only see those around me but acknowledge that I am
no better than they are.
May my voice be used to elevate the voiceless and to
speak out for those suffering injustice, in all forms.
May I listen with patience to those with whom I disagree, show mercy to all around me, and seek the nar-
row path of peace over the wide plains of war.
Lord, help to me never be ashamed to tell the world
that I am your child, and may I rest in the knowledge

that when I need the right words, your Spirit will descend upon me and give me the words of life. Help me to see how the Beatitudes are connected to each other, that no individual Beatitude can exist without the others. May I share the glory of your Gospel by my words, deeds, and actions. I ask this through Christ, our Lord. Amen.

DAY 17

....

My Day Begins

The work of the ordained minister, of the professional minister, is to enable the people of God to do the work of the Church. To feed us sacramentally—to enable us—to preach and to teach—and I ain't necessarily talking about preaching in the pulpit . . . as a Catholic Christian I have a responsibility to preach and teach, to worship and to pray. . .

The Church is calling us to be participatory and to be involved. The Church is calling us to feed and to clothe and to shelter and to teach. [32]

The Word of God became Incarnate. We are called to preach that word day by day by day—in our homes, in our families, in our neighborhood—to bear witness, to testify, to shout it from the rooftops, with our lives.[33]

All Through the Day

My soul has been anchored in the Lord.

My Day Is Ending

I, too, am called to evangelization in my own way and my identity is anchored in you. Father, I pray that you will reveal to me how I am being called to preach and to teach, how I am to worship and to pray.

When I was baptized, I became a member of your family. I was branded with your sign and I received a new name, just as Jacob became Israel or Simon became St. Peter.

As the waters of baptism touched my body, your Holy Spirit descended upon me, infusing me with the gifts of the Holy Spirit to be used for the common good. These gifts are nurtured by my living through and walking in virtue and your ways, and were sealed in me at Confirmation.

It is through the gifts of your Holy Spirit that I am able to bear good fruit. May I grow in wisdom, knowledge, counsel, fortitude, understanding, piety, and fear of you to better share the fruits of charity, joy, peace, patience, goodness, kindness, mildness, forbearance, fidelity, modesty, self-control, and chastity.

I know that as a member of your Church I am called to be your hands and feet in the world. Father, grant me your grace to always do your will in the world around me. Amen.

DAY 18

My Day Begins

Within the church, how can we work together so that all of us have equal access to input, equal access to opportunity, equal access to participation?

Go into a room and look around and see who's missing and send some of your folks out to call them in so that the Church can be what she claims to be, truly catholic.

Some black people don't approve of black religious expression in the Catholic liturgy. They've been told that it's not properly Catholic. They've been told that it's not appropriately serious or dignified or solemn or controlled, that the European way is necessarily the better way. . . .

All catechesis is supposed to be multicultural—but how little of it is. When we attempt to bring our black gifs to the church, people who do not know us say we are being "non-Catholic" or "Separatists" or just plain "uncouth."[34]

All Through the Day

There is no wrong way to worship the Lord.

My Day Is Ending

Father God, you have created us for expression and
you delight in variety.
May my worship of you be as varied as the flowers in
the field. Never let me believe the lie that there is only
one true way to worship you, because, if there were,
then you would have designed us to only worship in
one way.
May I worship you with my whole being, with my
voice, my thought, my actions, my soul. Father, I am
totally yours, may I dance for you like King David
danced for you. Amen.

DAY 19

∙∙

My Day Begins

Spirituality is conscious contract with the Spirit that is God, who is above us, who transcends and inspires us.

It is conscious contact with the spirit that is 'self,' with the inner-self where memory, imagination, intellect, feelings, and the body are caught up in the search for humanity. . . . Spirituality is at once God-awareness, self-awareness, and other-awareness. It is the level of consciousness and of choosing that makes us different from the pelican that dies on the beach and simply is no more.

Spirituality is faith lived.[35]

All Through the Day

My faith is the Holy Spirit living in me.

My Day Is Ending

Come Holy Spirit, enter into my heart, my mind, my soul, and infuse me with your inspiration.

Guide me along the path of what is good and true and beautiful. Help me to always remember that we are all part of your family of love and that we are all made in your divine image.

The words St. Paul shared with the Corinthians are also true for me: My body is a temple of the Holy Spirit, and my body is not my own. My body was purchased at a price when Jesus Christ, my Lord offered himself up as the spotless Lamb of God

for the forgiveness of my sins.

Make me into a dwelling place for you and help me to see that all bodies are good bodies. Able bodies, differently-abled bodies, thin bodies, fat bodies, tall bodies, small bodies, unborn bodies, light bodies, dark bodies, no matter the type of body, they are all temples of God.

Give me the strength to care for my body as a temple of God by discouraging unkind thoughts and behaviors. Help me to appreciate my body as your dwelling place by making wise choices to care for my body.

Help me to use this temple to effect positive change in the name of Jesus Christ in our world. May I always remember that *you* are at the center of my being and that you travel with me wherever I go, that you are alongside of me for all eternity. Amen.

DAY 20

●●●

My Day Begins

Each spiritual is in its own way a prayer—of yearning or celebration, of praise, petition, or contemplation, a simple lifting of heart, mind, voice, and life to God.

Black music reveals God as Protector, Creator, Sustainer of Life, Great Freedom-Fighter, Liberator, the Ultimate Source of Strength. The recurring affirmation is *God is* . . .

> He's a father to the fatherless,
>
> He's a mother to the motherless,
>
> He's a joy when you're in sorrow.
>
> He's your hope for tomorrow.

Black music speaks of God's creative love, infinite fidelity, vigilant protection, and eminent justice in a wealth of songs.

I did not realize that the songs would bring to me and to those I love comfort in sorrow, solace in grief, refuge in time of trouble, relief even from physical pain—always strength and hope, peace, and joy.[36]

All Through the Day

God is everything I need.

My Day Is Ending

Father, you welcomed me into your family when I was unworthy of your love and affection. You became my Father, Protector, Liberator, Strength, you became everything that I needed and everything that would ever need.

There are others in the world who are seeking a Father, Protector, Liberator, and Strength and they are looking everywhere but for you. St. Augustine put it well when he stated that our hearts are restless until they rest in you.

When someone shares with me what they are seeking and desiring, please send your Spirit with the words of life to invite them to attend Mass with me or to invite them to my home for a cup of coffee, tea, or to share a meal together.

Your Great Commission to us as your people was very clear in that we are called to share the Good News with everyone we meet so they can find their long-sought–after Father, Protector, Liberator, and Strength.

It is in you and through you that I become what you desire for me: that this image of God will be reunited and happy with you in heaven. Help me to see your image in those around me, my fellow brothers and sisters in Christ. Amen.

DAY 21

....

My Day Begins

Let the words and music speak to your whole soul, to your feelings, passions, and emotions. Feel what it means to have walked dry-shod though the Red Sea, to have placed your firstborn child in a manger, to have sat with Jesus by a well of Samaria, to have watched Jesus nailed upon a cross.

Pray with the song. Feel God's presence. Contemplate His goodness. Celebrate the Biblical theme in relationship to the daily mystery of God's working in your own life. Celebrate your own faith and hope and love. Pray in your own way. Move peacefully and gently as you feel drawn to discursive meditation or affective prayer or the contemplative prayer of simple resting in union with God.[37]

All Through the Day

My Soul is Glory-bound.[38]

My Day Is Ending

Father, sometimes prayer is hard, and everyone
has their own opinion on prayer. There are a lot of
"shoulds" out there when it comes to prayer: Prayer
should only be done in Latin. Prayer should only be
done in your native language. Prayer should only be
done kneeling or sitting or standing. Prayer should
only be done when you have enough time to do it right.
It is hard to know how I can talk to you. What should
I call you, as you have so many names? When I pray,
do you really hear me, or is someone more important
praying at the same time? I sometimes wonder if I
am praying wrong. . . . Is there is a right way to pray?
When you feel far from me, are you really gone?
But maybe you have so many names so that I always
know what to call you. You are my *Mighty Father,
Everlasting God, Wonderful, Counselor, Prince of Peace,
Emmanuel, Jesus.*
Your word reminds me that you will never leave my
side as you are my Shepherd and I am part of your
flock. Give me the confidence to know that no matter what others may think, the right way to pray is
the prayer that brings me closer to you and that you
delight in my reaching out to just say "Hi, Abba!" or
"Help me, Jesus!" or just "Thank You."

Thank you for always meeting me where I am and hearing my prayers no matter how I cry out to you. Help me to learn to let go and to let your Spirit move within me. Amen.

∙∙∙

My Day Begins

Now you know women can't preach in the Catholic Church. . . . I can't preach in the church. Women can't preach in the church. But I can preach in the streets. I can preach in the neighborhood. I can preach in the home. I can preach and teach in the family.

And it's the preaching that's done in the home that brings life and meaning to the Word your priest proclaims in his official ministry in the pulpit . . . when we honor the women, we honor you, too, men and children, because we honor your mothers and wives and lovers and sisters and daughters, aunts, and nieces, and friends. . . . [39]

I grew up with people who believed you could serve the Lord from a sickbed or death bed. The great commandment is to love the Lord your God with your whole heart, your whole soul, your whole mind, and all your strength. As long as I have my mental facility, I want to keep on loving. I want to keep on serving.

We're all called to preach, to shout the Good News by our lives. Never too young, never too old to share life, faith, and love . . . so long as we have breath and being, we are called to be life-givers and live-nourishers and life-sustainers.[40]

All Through the Day

I will keep busy serving my master God.

My Day Is Ending

Lord Jesus, just as St. Mary Magdalene shared the Good
News of your Resurrection with the apostles, you have
called me to share the Good News of your life, death,
and Resurrection with the world around me.
I may not be able to preach or teach but I can testify.
I can testify to your faithfulness, I can testify to your
goodness, I can testify to your saving grace that has set
me free.
I can testify that you are not a God of the past, but that
you are a God for all time, that you are still in the busi-
ness of saving and that every day you call us and you
send us forth with your life-giving words on our lips.
My authority to share this truth lies in you and I have
been gifted with the fullness of truth through our Holy
Mother Church. Forbid to me every fear of sharing the
news of your love with those around me, and may I
always share with a spirit of joy! Through Christ, who
lived, died, and rose for me. Amen.

DAY 23

••

My Day Begins

We are not all alike. Emphatically *no*! We do not look alike. We do not sing, dance, pray, play, think, cook, eat, wash, clean, chew, laugh, dress, or spit alike.

Asians are not like Europeans, are not like Africans. Irish are not like Italians, are not like French. Africans are not like Afro-Americans. Black folks are not alike. Folks from Louisiana are not like any other people in the world. Praise the Lord, we are not alike. If I begin to believe that we are all alike, look at what I'm going to miss: the richness, beauty, wholeness, and harmony of what God created.

The melting pot meant trying to develop a common culture according to the Euro-Caucasian model: black, red, brown, yellow, and all the other people were supposed to "get with it" and assimilate. They found themselves acceptable insofar as they sacrificed their ethical and cultural uniqueness.

The whole idea of a melting pot is unhealthy for people like me.

We think it's unhealthy for you, too.[41]

DAY 24

My Day Begins

You can be sure that Mary and Joseph were not ashamed of the stable in Bethlehem. They didn't choose it. They didn't ask for it. They knew they didn't deserve it. They let somebody else answer to God for the stable, while they thanked God for their child.

We've got to stop assuming all the blame and guilt for the failures of our people. We didn't shape human history by ourselves. For every opportunity we missed, another one was denied. And for every opportunity that was handed to us, we created another one ourselves. Oh, yes, we have plenty of reasons to plead for forgiveness, but we also have plenty of reasons to praise God with thanks.

God has spoken to the world through us. He has made himself present to the world through us. So we gather in God's house, just as Mary and Joseph did, to give praise with our thanksgiving. Knowing the wisdom of our ancestors who did with us what Mary and Joseph had done, we present our history and our lives before the altar and say thank you to God.[42]

All Through the Day

Thank you, my Lord and my God.

My Day Is Ending

Thank you, Jesus, for your sacrifice for me.
Even if I was the only living person on Earth, you
would have given your Body and Blood to redeem my
sins, allowing me entrance into your holy kingdom
when my time on Earth here is done. Lord, may I
never take for granted your selfless act of love.
It is really hard to put my will and my desires aside
for your will in my life, even though I know that your
will for me is infinitely greater than anything that I
could conceive on my own. When I choose to cast aside
instant gratification for myself to help make someone
else more comfortable, I am fulfilling my calling as a
Catholic. May I imitate your spirit of sacrifice in all that
I do for others and help me to be quick to forget that
act of service.
May all that I do be out of love for you and not for the
admiration of others. Jesus reminds us of the words
of the prophet Hosea when he said that God desires

My Day Is Ending

Father in heaven, when the mission here on Earth
seems overwhelming, please remind me that even
if one person comes to know, love, and serve you,
because my gift of self and the sharing of my witness,
so much good has taken place.
Your eternity is not an eternity of numbers, it is an
invitation to share in your love for all eternity.
Help me to always see the person standing before me
as an image of you, dear Lord. Remind me that those
with whom I disagree with here on Earth, through your
grace, I will be with them, praising you in heaven.
Just like your Son, Jesus, promised the repentant thief,
all of us who believe and profess that Jesus is Lord will
be united in heaven.
Help me to serve you with love, harmony, and hap-
piness, until you call me home. Through Christ, our
Lord. Amen.

DAY 27

My Day Begins

We become the miracle when we love one another.

Jesus says, "As the Father loves me, I love you." And "As I have loved you, love one another." He doesn't say love anyone that looks like you, thinks like you, prays like you, dresses like you, talks like you. "Love one another as I have loved you. Greater love than this nobody has than to lay down life."

Jesus said, "They will know that you are mine, because you love one another." When we love one another, we become the miracle. We witness to the miracle. We are transformed by his love, and the world beholds his glory in our transformation. [47]

It has to be love, love that overcomes fear, that shares and makes sure that nobody is hungry, that unites us when we learn about each other, when we share our gifts, when we believe in each other, when we take time to listen to each other, and to share our stories, our arts, our customs, our traditions, when we break bread together.[48]

All Through the Day

Bread is meant to be broken together.

My Day Is Ending

Dear Jesus, our story as your beloved creation is a story of love. It is a story of the love of self, of the love of neighbor, of the love of you.

Food is a language of love and when we break bread together, we are reminded of when you broke bread with your apostles one last time during the Passover celebration. When we share the eucharistic feast during the celebration of the Mass, we are united with all of the angels, saints, and Catholic Christians all around the world, saved by your selfless sacrifice.

Open my heart, ears, and eyes to see the goodness that comes from gathering together, and sharing meals with one another, especially when that sharing of a meal cannot be repaid in kind. Amen.

DAY 28

....

My Day Begins

My people used to say—and still say—sometimes you
have to moan. I remember old people sitting out on their
porches and moaning on and on in a kind of deep, melod-
ic hum. I've found that moaning is therapeutic. It's a way
of centering, the way you do in centering prayer. . . . Old
people used to say the words from Scripture, When we
don't know how to pray the Spirit intercedes for us with
inexpressible groaning.

Yes, I moan sometimes, I sing sometimes. When I'm
sick and don't have the internal resources to pray as I
would like, I sing or moan or hum. Because the songs are
so familiar, it is an easy way to pray, I find it goes away
when I hum or sing. . . . It's a lesson I learned from my
people and my heritage.[49]

All Through the Day

Oh, Mary, don't you weep, don't you mourn.[50]

My Day Is Ending

Father, may my words to you be words of praise.
May my songs to you be songs of celebration. May my
cries to you be cries of surrender and may my moans
be only understandable by you.

Lord, all I ask is that you hear and answer me, no matter the way that I pray.

Dearest Jesus, I seek you, I thirst for you, I long for
you, like a dry parched land devoid of all life-giving
water. May my lips glorify you, may my words be lifted
to you in praise, and may I find satisfaction and rest
only in you.

Presence of God, through your grace, may I leave
anger and rage behind and may I be comforted in the
shadow of your wings; create in me a clean heart, by
one drop of your blood, one drop of which is enough
to cleanse the world of her sins. Through Christ, our
Lord. Amen.

DAY 29

....

My Day Begins

I feel sometimes that I have something I want to do. I have something that I want to say before it's all over.

I'm a Franciscan. I want to be an instrument of peace. I want to be an instrument of hope. I want to be an instrument of faith and joy.

We are a pilgrim people traveling together in sorrow and joy toward that land of promise. Where there will be no more sorrow, no more moaning, no more weeping and wailing, no more good-bye, but just hello.

I want people to remember that I tried to love the Lord and that I tried to love them, and how that computes is immaterial.[51]

All Through the Day

We will understand it better by and by.[52]

My Day Is Ending

Lord God, when times are hard here on Earth, I take comfort in knowing that my time on Earth is finite and that this world is not the end for me.

While I am here on Earth, use me as your instrument for peace and understanding. May your words of forgiveness and love be experienced through what I say and what I do for and with others. Lord, keep me from becoming like the Pharisees, more concerned with following the letter of the law than with seeing you in the glory in the person standing before me.

And when death comes, allow me to see it not as a time of sorrow and fear but as the beginning of a new and glorious reunion with you, your Blessed Mother, all of the angels and saints, and with my loved ones who have gone on ahead of me.

I know that a day will come when there will be no more pain, no more weeping, only joy and praise of you, my Lord and my God, forever and ever. Amen.

DAY 30

My Day Begins

Poor little Jesus, born poor, born rejected, born far from home. . . . And even at His birth, loomed large the Shadow of the cross. He came to save the poor and lowly. He, in his flesh, has borne our sorrow. He became like us in all things but sin.[53]

All Through the Day

Jesus, Son of David, have mercy on me.

My Day Is Ending

Thank you, Lord Jesus, for in your birth, we are reborn.
Through your life, you teach us to life as you lived, to love as you loved. In your joy, we rejoice. In your sorrow, we weep. In our laughter, you delight. In our despair, you carry us. In your patience, we wait.

In your death, you bore our sorrow and you released us
from the icy-cold grip of death.
Through your resurrection, you reign victorious over
all of the powers of hell and you show us that the only
path to healing, restoration, and new life is
through you.
To you we give all the glory. *Gloria Patri, et Fili, et Spir-
itui Sancto. Sicut erat in principio, et nunc, et semper, in
saecula saeculorum.* Glory be to the Father, and the Son,
and the Holy Spirit. As it was in the beginning, is now
and ever shall be, world without end. Amen.

One Final Word

This book was created to be nothing more than a gateway—a gateway to the spiritual wisdom of a specific teacher and a gateway opening on your own spiritual way.

You may decide that Thea Bowman is someone whose experience of God is one that you wish to follow more closely and deeply, in which case you should get a copy of one of the books quoted in this text and pray it as you have prayed this gateway journey.

You may decide that this experience has heightened your hunger for additional spiritual teachers, and you will encounter many on your own, very special, absolutely unique journey of the spirit. You will discover your path. We would not be searching, as St. Augustine reminds us, if we had not already been found.

Permissions

Ave Maria Press is grateful to the following organizations who have allowed excerpts from Sr. Thea Bowman's writings and speeches to appear in the text:

Franciscan Sisters of Perpetual Adoration
fspa.org/content/about/sister-thea-bowman
United States Conference of Catholic Bishops
usccb.org
Pauline Books and Media
pauline.org

Notes

1. Thea Bowman, "Address to the U.S. Bishop's Conference," June 17, 1989. https://www.usccb.org/issues-and-action/cultural-diversity/african-american/resources/upload/Transcript-Sr-Thea-Bowman-June-1989-Address.pdf.

2. Aaron Mermelstein, director, *Sister Thea: Her Own Story* (Belleville IL: Oblate Media and Communications, 1991), videocassette, 93 minutes.

3. Bowman, *Almost Home: Living with Suffering and Dying* (Liguori, MO: Liguori Publishing Co, 1989), audiocassette.

4. "She Inspires Thousands, but Who Inspires Her?" *CUA Magazine* (Winter 1990), 7–9.

5. *Sister Thea: Songs of My People* (Boston: St. Paul Books and Media, 1989).

6. Civilla D. Martin, "His Eye Is On the Sparrow," 1905.

7. Bowman, "Address to the U.S. Bishop's Conference," June 17, 1989, https://www.usccb.org/issues-and-action/cultural-diversity/african-american/resources/upload/Transcript-Sr-Thea-Bowman-June-1989-Address.pdf.

8. Bowman, as quoted in "Experiencing Black Spirituality," selected and arranged by Lynne Holtzman, from *Thea Bowman: Handing On Her Legacy*, ed. Christian Koontz, R.S.M., 4. "Experiencing Black Spirituality" is drawn from Bowman's presentation at Mercy College of Detroit's "Second Conference on the Spiritual Woman: And Sarah Laughed" in April 1989.

9. Bowman, "Healing Ministry" speech at St. Stephen's Catholic Church, Minneapolis, MN, 1989. As quoted in *Thea Bowman: In My Own Words* by Maurice J. Nutt, C.Ss.R. (Liguori, MO: Liguori Press, 2009).

10. Bowman, speech at Milwaukee Martin Luther King Jr. celebration, January 17, 1988.

11. Bowman, "Let Us Love One Another during Holy Week," *Mississippi Catholic*, April 6, 1990.

12. Bowman, "Address to the U.S. Bishop's Conference" (June 17, 1989), https://www.usccb.org/issues-and-action/cultural-diversity/african-american/resources/upload/Transcript-Sr-Thea-Bowman-June-1989-Address.pdf.

13. Bowman, "Black History and Culture," *U.S. Catholic Historian*, 7, nos. 2 and 3. Spring/Summer 1989, 307–310.

14. Bowman, "Black History and Culture," *U.S. Catholic Historian,* 7, nos. 2 and 3. Spring/Summer 1989, 307–310.

15. Bowman, *Families: Black and Catholic, Catholic and Black*, Washington, DC: United States Catholic Conference, 1985.

16. *Sister Thea: Songs of My People* (Boston: St. Paul Books and Media, 1989).

17. Aaron Mermelstein, director *Sister Thea: Her Own Story* (Belleville, IL: Oblate Media and Communications, 1991), videocassette, 93 minutes.

18. "This Little Light of Mine" is a popular hymn, and the lyrics' origins are unknown. Harry Dixon Loes created a widely published and recorded arrangement in the 1940s.

19. Bowman, interview by Joe Smith, *Smith and Company,* WMTV Madison WI, January 18, 1988, and Aaron Mermelstein, director *Sister Thea: Her Own Story* (Belleville IL: Oblate Media and Communications, 1991), videocassette, 93 minutes.

20. *Sister Thea: Songs of My People* (Boston: St. Paul Books and Media, 1989).

21. *Sister Thea: Songs of My People* (Boston: St. Paul Books and Media, 1989).

22. *Sister Thea: Songs of My People* (Boston: St. Paul Books and Media, 1989).

23. Thomas Dorsey, "Precious Lord, Take My Hand," © 1938, Unichappell Music, Inc. (renewed). Assigned to Warner-Tamerlane Publishing Corporation.

24. Bowman, interview by Joe Smith, *Smith and Company*, WMTV Madison, WI, January 18, 1988, and Bowman's presentation at Mercy College of Detroit's "Second Conference on the Spiritual Woman: And Sarah Laughed" in April 1989.

25. Bowman, "Black History and Culture," *U.S. Catholic Historian,* 7, nos. 2 and 3. Spring/Summer 1989, 307–310.

26. Bowman, *Families: Black and Catholic, Catholic and Black*, Washington, DC: United States Catholic Conference, 1985.

27. Bowman, Families: *Black and Catholic, Catholic and Black*, Washington, DC: United States Catholic Conference, 1985.

28. Bowman, *Families: Black and Catholic, Catholic and Black*, Washington, DC: United States Catholic Conference, 1985.

29. Bowman, "Address to the U.S. Bishop's Conference," June 17, 1989, https://www.usccb.org/issues-and-action/cultural-diversity/african-american/resources/upload/Transcript-Sr-Thea-Bowman-June-1989-Address.pdf.

30. Speech at St. Clement Pope Church, as quoted in *Sister Thea Bowman, Shooting Star: Selected Writings and Speeches*, ed. Celestine Cepress, F.S.P.A. St. Mary's Press, 1993, 78.

31. "Every Time I Feel the Spirit" is a traditional hymn whose author remains unknown.

32. Bowman, "Address to the U.S. Bishop's Conference," June 17, 1989, https://www.usccb.org/issues-and-action/cultural-diversity/african-american/resources/upload/Transcript-Sr-Thea-Bowman-June-1989-Address.pdf.

33. Bowman, speech at St. Clement Pope Church, as quoted in *Shooting Star,* 78.

34. Bowman, "Address to the U.S. Bishop's Conference," June 17, 1989, https://www.usccb.org/issues-and-action/cultural-diversity/african-american/resources/upload/Transcript-Sr-Thea-Bowman-June-1989-Address.pdf.

35. Bowman, "Spirituality: The Soul of the People" from *Tell It Like It Is: A Black Catholic Perspective on Christian Education* (Oakland, CA: National Black Sisters' Conference [NBSC], 1983, 84–85).

36. Bowman, "Spirituality: The Soul of the People" from *Tell It Like It Is: A Black Catholic Perspective on Christian Education* (Oakland, CA: National Black Sisters' Conference [NBSC], 1983, 84–85).

37. *Sister Thea: Songs of My People* (Boston: St. Paul Books and Media, 1989).

38. J. R. Baxter and Clyde McClain "Jesus Is Mine." Copyright © 1945 Bridge Building Music (BMI) (adm. at CapitolCMGPublishing.com) All rights reserved. Used by permission.

39. Speech at St. Clement Pope Church, as quoted in *Shooting Star*, 76–77.

40. Bowman, "Lord, Let Me Live Till I Die," interview with Fabvienen Taylor, *Praying* (Nov.–Dec. 1989), 19–22.

41. Reflection found in Bowman's unpublished papers and as quoted in *Shooting Star*, 84-85.

42. Bowman, speech at St. Columba Church, as quoted in *Shooting Star*, 90–91.

43. Bowman, "Religious and Cultural Variety: Gift to Catholic Schools" from *The Non-Catholic in the Catholic School*, Washington, DC: National Catholic Educational Association, 1984 and 1987, 20–25.

44. Bowman, "She Inspires Thousands, but Who Inspires Her?" *CUA Magazine*, Winter 1990, 7–9.

45. Bowman, interview by Joe Smith, *Smith and Company,* WMTV Madison WI, January 18, 1988.

46. Bowman, as quoted in Lyn L. Hartman, "The Message of Music," *Milwaukee Journal,* Jan 17, 1988.

47. Bowman, "Cosmic Spirituality: No Neutral Ground," as appears in *Formation in a New Age: Proceedings of the 1997 Religious Formation National Congress.*

48. Bowman, "Trusting the Prophetic Call," interview with Catherine Browning, *Creation* (Nov.—Dec. 1989), 19–21.

49. Bowman, "Lord, Let Me Live Till I Die," interview with Fabvienen Taylor, *Praying* (Nov.—Dec. 1989), 19–22.

50. "O Mary, Don't You Weep" is a traditional hymn whose author remains unknown.

51. Mermelstein, Aaron, director *Sister Thea: Her Own Story* (Belleville IL: Oblate Media and Communications, 1991), videocassette, 93 minutes.

52. Charles Albert Tindley, "We'll Understand It Better By and By," ca. 1906.

53. *Sister Thea: Songs of My People* (Boston: St. Paul Books and Media, 1989).

Servant of God Sr. Thea Bowman (1937–1990) joined the Franciscan Sisters of Perpetual Adoration in La Crosse, Wisconsin, when she was fifteen years old. Bowman developed a deep appreciation for her identity as fully Black and fully Catholic and became a poet, preacher, master teacher, vocalist, evangelist, and prophetic voice for change and renewal across the United States.

She earned her master's degree and doctorate at the Catholic University of America, then taught at CUA, Viterbo College, and Xavier University.

Just before her death in 1990, the University of Notre Dame announced that Bowman would receive the Laetare Medal, which is given to a Catholic "whose genius has ennobled the arts and sciences, illustrated the ideals of the Church and enriched the heritage of humanity."

Bowman's cause for canonization was endorsed by the US bishops in 2018 and is ongoing.

www.sistertheabowman.com

Karianna Frey is a Catholic writer, speaker, and ministry leader. She is a member of the Fiat Conference planning team and the author of two books, *Serviam Non Serviam* and *The Virtuous Path*.

www.kariannafrey.com
Instagram: @kariannafrey